Better not Broken

a practical, positive guidebook for divorce

Sara Jacobs

Printed in the United States of America
Published by Braughler Books LLC., Springboro, Ohio

First printing, 2021

ISBN: 978-1-955791-05-2 soft cover
ISBN: 978-1-955791-06-9 ebook

Library of Congress Control Number: 2021919105

Ordering information: Special discounts are available on quantity purchases by bookstores, corporations, associations, and others. For details, contact the publisher at:

sales@braughlerbooks.com

or at 937-58-BOOKS

For questions or comments about this book, please write to:

info@braughlerbooks.com

Braughler™
Books
braughlerbooks.com

This book is full of down to earth common sense stuff that is so helpful for someone just starting the process. Too many other books have too much gobbledygook to really help. This guidebook is short and concise. I found the chapter "New Life – New You" especially helpful because you need to hear that you should get to know yourself again and focus on yourself after the marriage ends.

Kay – Franklin North, Carolina

This book saved me so much money and time with my attorney. The chapters about kids and parenting plans made such a positive difference in what my ex and I put together. AND it gave me real life strategies for being a better parent and how to support my kids through the process and keep moving forward. As hard as it was, we really are Better not Broken.

Erin – Cincinnati

Dedication

Divorce can be tough, make no mistake about that. But imagine how daunting the process would be in the North American colonies in the 17th Century. Yet, on January 5, 1643, in the Massachusetts Bay Colony Anne Clarke was granted a divorce from her husband Denis Clarke who had abandoned her and their children to start a new life with another woman. Hers was the first divorce granted in colonial North America. When I imagine the harshness of life in the winter of 1643 in Massachusetts the lack of plumbing, electricity and central heating alone would be enough to keep me in my house. Add to that the position of women at this time in history, and I think Anne must have been a truly plucky woman of genuine courage. This guidebook is dedicated to her, who though she left nothing behind but this tiny footnote in history, is an inspiration to me and an example of the need and positive value of divorce.

Contents

A Guidebook for Divorce

*"And I think that's important, to know how the
water's gone over the dam before you start to describe it.
It helps to have been over the dam yourself."*

— E. ANNIE PROULX

*"Don't follow any advice no matter how good,
until you feel as deeply in your spirit as you
think in your mind that the counsel is wise."*

— JOAN RIVERS

Smart travelers do their research before heading off to a place they
have never been. Every journey can benefit from a guidebook that
explains the customs, the people, the culture, the highlights, and
the places to avoid. Divorce is better understood as a place many of
us visit while on the journey of our lives, rather than a descriptor of
who we are. And like all travel it has the potential to change your
life both positively and negatively. Being prepared and having a
good guidebook will increase your chances of your divorce being
a good experience.

Traveling through the land of divorce can be scary and lonely,
it can also be freeing and invigorating: it will absolutely hold
some surprises, not all of them bad. Sure, you can plunge into the
unknown without a guidebook and wing it, see where you end up;
but there is a lot to be said for using guidebook that will keep you
from taking some wrong turns or making big mistakes. Trust me
on this, I took those turns and I made so many of those mistakes.

The other thing smart travelers do is to give consideration to
all the aspects of their trip, prior starting out, and again during
the trip. They manage the budget, the time, the accommodations,

their traveling companions, the things they will bring along. This is so they can get the most out of the experience; and they adjust their course along the way if something goes wrong or new opportunities appear. This same sort of management is needed when you are going through divorce and for the same reason, to get the most out of the experience. In this guidebook you will find information to help you manage the different aspects of the divorce process: your soon to be ex, attorneys, money, housing, your children, your emotions, your expectations, and the new life you will be creating as you go through the process. Sometimes the best thing you can do to manage a situation is to simply step back and take a deep breath and wait for a difficult situation to pass. Other times managing will require you to dig deep and find courage you didn't know you have. Prepare yourself, because there will be difficult moments when the smartest way to manage is to shut your mouth, keep your opinions to yourself and ignore the advice and counsel of friends and family members. Another thing I learned the hard way.

Despite all the advances of our modern culture and society our view of divorce and the people and families who go through divorce is still very often old fashioned and unenlightened. We as a culture still, subtly or not so subtly, place a negative mark next to the individuals and the children who have been through divorce, characterizing them as "broken". It is a truth that we are quick to rush people down the aisle into marriage, but not so keen on supporting or helping when the marriage has come to be more like a slow death rather than a lifegiving foundation to the lives of the people involved.

Whole, functioning couples don't divorce. The couples who decide to end their marriages and divorce do so precisely because the marriage is no longer a place that is functioning well and creating a home life where the people can thrive. The truly ironic thing here is that most people who divorce do so, not seeking to break something in their lives, but in fact to restore wholeness to their lives and subsequently the lives of their children. Couples who divorce are seeking to become whole because living in the marriage is breaking them.

Perhaps the most daunting or even terrifying thing that keeps people from even thinking about, much less engaging, in divorce is the idea that you will be ruining the lives of your children. If I had a dollar for every person who said they were staying married "for the kids" and another dollar for each kid who said, "wish you had done it sooner," I would be a very rich person. If you have convinced yourself that living unhappily or stunted or in silence with your spouse in the same house "married" is showing your kids the best way to be in a committed, *healthy* relationship you are wrong. If you believe that the only way to show a child love and stability is in a "married" household, again you are living with a misconception.

A major responsibility of being a parent is modeling and teaching your children how to make and keep healthy relationships. Exposure to constant fighting, long, cold, hostile silences, infidelity, acting out financially or acting out in other ways does not prepare your child for choosing a good partner and making their own good marriage. Plus, as a child it is not fun to grow up in a hostile environment. And if you are telling yourself that because you and your spouse do not openly argue in front of the kids, but just silently seethe against each other, that all is well for the kids, again, you are wrong.

If you are considering getting divorced or already in the process of divorce, this guidebook is for you. Divorce is all around us (40-50% of marriages in the United States end) but most of us know nothing about it until we are in the middle of it many of us in the emotional deep end of the pool flailing. I have been in that deep end more than most.

I have been married twice and divorced twice, and I am a true romantic. I believe in romance and marriage and healthy relationships that create and support the individuals and families. I also believe very strongly that bad, sad marriages are best ended for the good of everyone, including and especially the kids. (I know I am not supposed to say this, but it's true). But I don't want you just to get through your divorce, I want you to come out on the other side into your new life, a better you, stronger healthier and bringing your kids up in two great homes!

When I made the decision to divorce over 20 years ago, I found myself in a very lonely place with almost no resources or information about how to divorce. I would sneak into the self-help section of bookstores looking for guidance and reassurance, any kind of light or lifeline. There were dozens of books about marriage and relationships and plenty on divorce, but they were too long and intense and only overwhelmed and depressed me. I was struggling just to get through the day. I had two small children, a part-time job, and every day I felt like I was drowning and losing myself in this unhappy life. What I needed was good, solid information and advice in digestible amounts from a source I could trust. I was searching for hope and guidance. Unfortunately, there was little to be found.

This guide will help you navigate through the divorce process and into your new life. It is designed to help you find your way so that you can travel through the process and come out the other side a better person. You will find here simple, honest advice to help you and your family become better by the process, not broken.

Because of the isolation I experienced I have spoken openly and positively about my divorce as a way to reach out to others who are going through this process. These conversations help to put people at ease and feel less alone as well as contribute to normalizing rather than ostracizing people who experience divorce. I have met so many people just like I was, contemplating divorce who were terrified because they didn't know how it works or where to start. Others I have met were in the process but were at their wits' end trying to understand it all or had thrown up their hands discouraged and exhausted by the process and were no longer able to advocate for the best choices for themselves and their children.

Divorce seems so easy on television or in conversation, "just get divorced"; but when you decide it's time to actually make the move, it can be truly daunting. I am sure there are thousands of couples who spend much longer than is necessary or healthy, in their unhappy marriages simply because the process to divorce seems so confusing and negative. They already feel exhausted and crushed, divorce seems just too much, so they stay unhappy.

This guidebook is about inspiring you and informing you. It contains straight forward, simple information you that will ease your mind, boost your courage, and help you get started. There is also advice on how to navigate the process and get your life up and running post-divorce.

Pick a section and you will find basic information and guidance. You won't find everything that you will need to know, the laws of divorce vary from place to place and there are countless variations to each particular divorce making it impossible to address everything you will need to know and deal with. But it will give you a solid foundation and I hope a boost of "can do!". What is here is based on my own experience going through the divorce process and what I have learned from others who shared their experiences with me.

I am addressing those divorces that do not include abuse and illegal activities. If your spouse is truly abusing you and your children, physically, emotionally, and/or financially, seek professional help now. This book can give you basic information you can use, but if you are dealing with grave and disabling abuse, you will need more professional expertise and guidance to secure the best way out of your marriage; especially if you have children.

It is important to understand that divorce is not the break. Divorce is the process you undertake to fix the break and bring about the end of a marriage that is not lifegiving, so you can begin to live fully. It is the legal process and social ritual that we go through to be officially and officially released from a marriage; a marriage that for whatever reasons, is no longer able to support the couple, and, by association the children, in a loving and supportive and healthy manner.

Gather your courage and take heart! You can do this! You and your children will not become permanently broken humans. Yes, there will be tough moments, days, weeks, even months and there will be changes and challenges, lots of them, (some of them will be wonderful and unexpected and fun!). But the changes and challenges of this process most often foster growth, not brokenness. And if you are being honest, isn't your nonworking marriage offering up significant challenges and tough days (maybe even some truly ugly surprises) with little or no hope for things getting better? If you are wishing that your spouse would die in a freak accident, so that you can be free, (admit it, you probably have thought this) then it's probably time to seriously consider divorce and get going on a new start to make life whole again.

Divorce is a place, a pass through on your life's journey. It isn't your life's one defining moment though you may find some defining moments along the way. And it isn't a personality trait, like hair color or height, though people may try to assign it to you as if it is. Nor it isn't a brand or a tattoo, though you just may acquire a badge of honor.

This is your guidebook through the land of divorce. Manage yourself and travel well, you can do this and you will be better for it.

CHAPTER 1

The Decision

*"Full maturity ... is achieved by
realizing you have choices to make."*
— Angela Deavere Smith

*"Say you were standing with one foot in the oven
and one foot in an ice bucket. According to the
percentage people, you would be perfectly comfortable."*
— Bobby Bragan

If you are reading this you have either decided to divorce, are strongly considering a divorce or have been presented with your spouse's decision to divorce. The decision to divorce, like the decision to marry ushers you into a process and rituals that lead you into a new life. For most people, the decision to marry was made by two people, happily, with plans for a great future grounded in the marriage. It was probably discussed thoroughly and thoughtfully, and every detail of the wedding carefully considered. The decision to divorce is usually less collaborative and happy; sometimes one partner is not even aware that the decision is being made. The social response to these two life changes is also radically different. Announce your engagement and you can expect a shower of good wishes; announce your divorce and brace yourself for a tidal wave of silence.

If you are contemplating divorce, the best-case scenario is to be in that tiny group of couples who for whatever reason wake up one day and decide that they don't want to be married anymore. They agree mutually that the marriage is not working, and quickly sort and settle their assets and debts and move on. But this is an itty-bitty number of the couples who divorce. For most couples there is a period of agonizing over the decision that can last weeks, months, years and sadly sometimes decades. A breakdown has occurred between you and your spouse and the voice in your head that used to call you to repair and keep going has been replaced by a voice that says, "this isn't working, it's never going to work again, I would be better off without this marriage." The images of a happy you that play in your head no longer include your spouse.

Getting divorced is a monumental decision, and just like the decision to get married, it will change the course of your life. If you have made the decision to divorce, you know that change is coming, and you want that. You know that your marriage, as a healthy union, is over, and you want to end it officially. The promises you made and the future that you committed to no longer exists and cannot be resurrected.

If you are on the receiving end of the decision, your spouse has asked you for a divorce or told you that you are getting one. This may come as a complete surprise leaving you feeling like your world has been shattered, and in fact it has. But for most, even if your spouse is the one to ask for the divorce, there is probably some awareness that something has changed between the two of you and not for the better. Regardless of your awareness level, something has brought your spouse to this point of calling it quits and officially ending the marriage. You certainly are entitled to an explanation, to your anger, to tears, but if your spouse is truly ready to end things, acceptance is going to move you along faster and better to the next chapter of your life. It is a tough blow and by all means, have some good long cries, toss a few plates, slams some doors, spend some time in complete shock and fear.

But then, take a deep breath, gather your strength, dig deep, and start to envision your future ahead. Even the spouse who is taken completely by surprise, upon grasping the reality that they are no longer loved and cherished by this person, will more likely have a brighter future ahead.

This is a guidebook about how to divorce, not how to save your marriage, but part of the process before the attorneys are engaged is to make sure that you are sure this is the right choice.

There are all sorts of things that can bring a marriage to a place that it can no longer be revived or salvaged. For most marriages that end there are multiple issues at play: infidelity, financial trouble, physical or mental health issues, changes in shared goals. It may be your own or your spouse's personal growth and changes that result in you no longer being in synch with your hopes and dreams for life. But marriages can and do survive these and many other challenges, so before you embark on the path of divorce, scour your mind and your heart and be sure that you do not see a healthy resolution to whatever the particular issues are in your marriage that have brought you here.

There is an enormous difference between being married as it is intended to be and staying in a dead marriage simply to stay married. The most important first step in the divorce process is to make sure that you have done all that you can to make the marriage work. Being able to say to that voice in your head, or your children or your family and friends, that you did everything you could to make it work is important. The day will come when you are wondering if it was the right thing, the "what ifs?" will pop up and it is vital that you can answer them with conviction that you did all you could to make your marriage succeed. Being honest with yourself will help you through this process and help you in your future relationships.

Many people seek divorce because they have come to believe that the problem in the marriage and the problem in their life, is the other person, and divorce, by getting rid of the other person in your life, will solve the problems. It is amazingly easy and feels really good, to blame your spouse for all or most of the problems in your marriage. And there certainly are instances where one person carries more fault for the failure of the marriage. However, to make the right decision, you must be willing to look at yourself and what you are doing in the marriage as well. Perhaps you have experienced changes that have led you away from your spouse and the vision and values you once shared, or maybe you have found someone else. If this is the case, own those realities. People change, it is one of the few constants in life, but we don't always change in a way that meshes with or compliments our spouse, especially since that person is changing too.

If your partner has found a new partner, that is a deep and painful wound, and you will have to work extremely hard to keep that anger and bitterness in check during the divorce process. Find an outlet for your feelings but raging at your soon to be ex either publicly or privately, no matter how much they may deserve it, won't help with the process. The best response toward them, is silence on this topic and it will save you potentially ugly and embarrassing scenes. If your partner is calling an end to what has become an unhealthy or lifeless marriage, as hard as it may be, consider being grateful that someone has pulled the trigger.

Whatever your situation is, if you can get professional counseling, either alone or together do it. The value of some clarity from the perspective of an objective professional cannot be overstated. Don't skip over this because you think you will be plunged into an endless torment of therapy sessions. You may be surprised at what comes out in therapy. You may find things you suspected confirmed, and quickly conclude that divorce is the best route for you. Being in the room with an objective professional to guide the discussion can produce more truth and clarity in a few sessions than the two of you acting out or acting passively aggressive will conjure in an entire year. If your partner has presented you with the divorce and they are not willing to work on things, there is really nothing you can do. In some instances, the other person will simply refuse to try again or go to counseling. Stalling or refusing to move forward will only make the bad situation worse, escalating anger and bitterness.

If you are among the lucky few who have come to this decision amicably and mutually, use that to your advantage. You may be able to do much of the heavy lifting of the process between the two of you and perhaps even utilize only one attorney.

Finally, if you have been talking and sharing your unhappiness and the anguish of the decision with your friends, now is the time to limit those discussions and the number of people that you are talking to about this if you are truly going to take the step to divorce. Why? Because people talk, and people talking about other people's relationships don't always get it right and don't keep it to themselves. Your divorce process will be much smoother and less painful if neither you nor your spouse are hearing about yourselves at the school open house or a neighborhood cookout. When you have made the decision, show some maturity, and share it with your spouse and children before you share it with all your friends and family.

Once the decision is made, or accepted, you are on a new path, toward a new life. The best decisions, even the most painful ones, can set you on the path to a fuller, healthier, better life.

Key Management Points

- Explore every reasonable avenue to fix the problems in the marriage. The goal being a happy productive relationship, not just a tolerable existence.

- If the other person is presenting the decision of divorce to you and it is a final decision, accept it and get an attorney, fighting it will most likely only have negative effects.

- Accept that all aspects of your life are going to change.

- Get an attorney unless you and your spouse are in total agreement about ending the marriage.

CHAPTER 2

Change

*"One must never lose time in vainly regretting the
past or in complaining against the changes which
cause us discomfort, for change is the essence of life."*
— ANATOLE FRANCE

*"Only in growth, reform and change,
paradoxically enough, is true security to be found."*
— ANNE MORROW LINDBERGH

The bedrock truth life is that life is always changing. You have been
changing since the day you were born. Change must happen for
life to move forward, try to imagine it otherwise. What rattles us
about change is that it makes us feel out of control and fearful. Even
changes you initiate, or welcome can make you uncomfortable with
a sense of not being in control. But the truth is, with most of life,
you actually have extraordinarily little control. What you are able
to do is find a way to stave off the fear. So, take a deep breath, and
realize that while you cannot stop change, you can decide how you
are going to respond to it.

Like it or not, ready, or not, when you divorce the course of your
life is set in a new direction. Change is truly the essence of divorce.
All aspects of your life will be affected on all levels. Which is not to
say it will all be negative. Some changes will be great and will bring
rise to more good change. Even if you are the person who initiated
the divorce, and you think you know what changes lie ahead, be
prepared. Change on this scale will have a domino effect in your
life and it will take a great deal of energy and attention to manage.
Be patient and gentle with yourself, and with the others involved.

People react to change in different ways and most have multiple ways of responding to change. When you are going through divorce there will be days when all you want to do is throw a blanket over your head and hide. Other days you will want to rage against everything, and everyone involved in the divorce. And some days you will find yourself utterly joyful with the prospect of your new life ahead. All of these are understandable and to be expected and accepted. Work to establish an equilibrium of dealing with these changes, bouncing too high and too low overtime is not only exhausting, but also disorienting to you and those around you. Too low too often will cloud your strength and focus. Too high too often can result in you not taking the proper time to recognize what is happening and grieve the end of what at one time was the most meaningful relationship in your life. Go ahead and have the mini breakdown, do the happy dance all through the house; then gather yourself together and adopt a stance of calm acceptance of change and a positive approach to the challenges ahead. Start finding for the benefits of the changes coming your way. As much as they may look and feel negative, and some of them are, do yourself a favor and create a positive platform for assessing and responding to them.

A big positive thing about the changes coming your way via the divorce, is that you can see some of them coming and so to a certain extent, you can prepare and plan.

As you transition from a married person to a single person, your responsibilities and obligations will shift. You will have more responsibilities and decision-making power in the management of your finances, parenting, household, automobiles, healthcare, entertainment, free time, all sorts of places. Some of these will be changes you have longed for, and others...well, others you may have never ever wanted! The good news is you don't have to face all of this change alone. If you are feeling fearful as you take on something new, ask a friend or relative for help or to be with you.

Divorced means "not married," it doesn't mean "consigned to deal with life alone."

Prepare to be overwhelmed but also be ready and open to conquering the tasks that come with this new life. For many people just the thought of buying a car, much less a house on their own is overwhelming. In these instances, take a deep breath; people all around you are doing these things and you can too. Not sure how to start? Go online, buy a book, consult a professional. The feeling of accomplishment you get when you tackle a life decision or skill that is out of your comfort zone is amazing! Don't be surprised if the first time you replace a toilet seat, change the oil on the lawn mower, or purchase a power tool you find yourself walking around like a DIY master! Buy a house on your own? Real estate mogul!

Very few people have the life they thought they would have exactly as they planned. Plans are made to be changed and are best understood as guides rather than sure things. It isn't always easy or possible to face the changes coming your way with grace and good cheer but it sure will make life better when you do.

Key Management Points

- Change is a constant in life, you cannot stop it. Learn to embrace it.

- Many of the changes that come with divorce are positive.

- How you make it through all this change is up to you and how you choose to manage it. We have much more control over our emotional management than most of us think.

- Sometimes you need to adopt an emotional stance that is open and accepting to change even when you are terrified. "Fake it till you make it" is a great place to start.

CHAPTER 3

Attorneys

"Fools and obstinate people make rich lawyers."
— Proverb

First and foremost, understand the role of your attorney in your divorce. Your attorney is your expert in the laws of your locale who will act as a guide through the system. Attorneys are businesspeople, and your divorce is the business; the end of your marriage is their business opportunity. Keep in mind that as compassionate and caring as she or he is, the only reason you are dealing with this person is to accomplish your divorce. Going through divorce can be lonely and isolating, and there may be times when you feel your attorney is the only one who understands what you are going through. Unless you are in the habit of paying for friendship, remember that every time you talk to this person you are **paying for the conversation**. You don't want to learn this the expensive way by getting a bill for a conversation that you thought was more a friendly exchange than a working call. When responding to your attorney's inquiries, be brief and direct and stick to business. When you feel the need to pour your heart out call a close confidant and talk to them; they won't send you a bill.

That being said, unless you are in a very agreeable position with your spouse on the matter of divorce, you are better off going through the divorce process with an attorney. The laws, rules, and regulations governing divorce vary in every state and even county to county. You need an attorney who knows and understands those regulations where you are divorcing who then will act as your guide through the process.

It is best to engage an attorney and commit to the process before you begin announcing to people that you are getting divorced. This gives you some solid footing and understanding before people jump in with their own "advice" and experiences. People mean well, but often don't have real knowledge or may for their own reasons try to discourage you from moving ahead.

It is important to hire someone with whom you can be completely honest about all aspects of your marriage. It can be awkward initially to share the intimate and possibly ugly and embarrassing workings of your life with a stranger, but you will get used to it. Relax, these are professionals who spend their days looking at people's lives. You probably won't present anything they haven't seen before, and most of them have good poker faces; so even if you bring some real crazy, they are going to keep a cool front. Not being honest and giving a full picture will work against you. The better your attorney understands your situation, the better advocate they can be toward accomplishing your goals.

Look for someone who is efficient and will be honest with you about the process and what is and is not achievable in your case. It is a scary thing to find an attorney when you are already so emotionally shaken. Look online and interview a few over the phone or in person or get references from people who have been through the process but do your research before you put down your retainer. Most of us would spend as much time as it takes to find the right pair of shoes, so take the time to find the right attorney.

You are going to have to trust this person and take the advice they give, which won't always be what you want to hear, so be sure that the attorney you engage is someone whose guidance and counsel you will follow. Asking questions to understand the process is essential but pushing back because you don't like what you hear will cost you time and therefore money. These people are professionals and have seen so many divorces and circumstances that they will have foresight and insight that you do not have and that you need. Listen to your attorney.

Once you sign on with an attorney the divorce will go from theoretical swirling in your head to REAL LIFE. It isn't that there is no turning back after meeting with a lawyer, the process can be stopped at any time. But once you meet with the attorney, the process will start to move forward and the reality that this is what you are doing – GETTING DIVORCED – becomes clear and real.

How It Works

Your Billing Statement from Ms Attorney X

Date	Service	Time	Charge
7/14	Call with client	45 min @ $300.00 ph	225.00
7/14	Call with opposing counsel	30 min @ $300.00 ph	150.00
7/15	Call with client	1 hour @ $300.00 ph	300.00
7/15	Call with opposing counsel	10 min @ $300.00 ph	75.00
		Administrative fees: copies and mailings	50.00
		Total	800.00

When it comes to attorneys, TIME IS MONEY and attorneys are billing by the minute. Here is how it works. When you decide on an attorney, you will be required to pay a retainer fee. A retainer is a lump sum that you pay before any work is done on your divorce. Retainers are usually in the amount of $1500 - $5000 depending on the complexity of your situation. The attorney will then bill against this amount until it runs out. If it runs out and your divorce is not complete, you will be required to pay more. If you wrap things up quickly and there is money left, that is returned to you. You can expect to be billed in quarter hour increments for your attorney's time spent with you or working on your case as well as meetings and phone calls with the other attorney, court fees, clerical and administrative work such as copies and mail. It adds up quickly, so anything you can do to limit time spent do it.

You can see that it adds up quickly, so it is 1000% in your best interest to be efficient in your dealings with your attorney. If this explanation of retainers and billing has freaked you out and scared you out of proceeding, remember that thousands of people divorce with less means than you. It is daunting when you begin understanding the process, but people manage it all the time. Don't let the cost scare you out of making this move if this is the right move for you. If you don't have the funds for an attorney readily available, you can put it on a credit card or borrow from a family member. There is a cost to this, but the cost of unhappy living is much higher for all.

Even though you have an attorney to do the business of dealing with your soon to be ex and the ending of your marriage, **the truth is the other business partner in this process is your soon to be ex-spouse.** Now that you understand how attorneys charge for their services, you can see that anything you and your spouse can agree on outside of the lawyers' offices or meetings will be money that stays in your pockets. You may think you will not be able to agree on much, but you will probably both agree that you would rather keep more money to divide for your futures than pay more to the attorneys. Breathe deep, maybe even swallow some pride, or eat some crow, and see if you can find a way to work together to limit the time and money drain from the attorneys.

Sometimes the anger and emotions are running so high that people look for an attorney who will be a "ball buster" or will "destroy" the other person. This level of engagement takes more time and consequently more money. And if those are your goals, seriously reexamine them, especially if you have children. The goal of divorce is to end the marriage so that both parties to move on in life, not to cripple one another.

Conversely many people are so fearful of the conflict and arguments that they see looming in the process that they opt for the "collaborative process" that is often advertised as an amicable way to divorce, not unlike the amicable way you married. Be very wary of this process. It has meetings and steps built into it that that may make the process take longer or may not work at all. Then you will have to start over with new attorneys which is more cost. The choice to be amicable and work together lies with you, not your attorneys or the name of the process. If you and your spouse are truly in an amicable place, consider enlisting the services of one attorney. It is a small number of people who fit into this category, but if you do, take advantage of it.

The bottom line on this is that you need an attorney who will work as your guide and manager through the process. AND you need to do all you can to manage yourself so that the process goes as positively as possible and you can get on with your life.

Key Management Points

- The laws of divorce vary widely; from state to state and even county to county.

- Hire an attorney who is knowledgeable and efficient.

- Time is money. Manage your interactions with your attorney to keep down cost.

- Be prepared to take the advice of your attorney.

CHAPTER 4

Negotiating and Settling

*"I make the most of all that comes
and the least of all that goes."*

—Sara Teasdale

"If you can't fight and you can't flee, flow."

—Robert Eliot

Once you and your spouse have engaged attorneys the legal side of the process is fully in motion and it is game on. This is where things get real. You will need to take deep breaths, long naps or do whatever it is that helps you to remain calm as things move along. One meeting with your attorney may go great and the next feels like you are falling into a black hole. Stay calm, you are in for the marathon not the sprint.

You and your spouse are enmeshed, financially and materially and through your children. Your attorneys are going to work with you to create a document that separates you so that you can both stand alone. You are not going to get everything you want. Read that again. *You are NOT going to get everything you want.* But rather than dwell on that, take the time to determine what are the things you really do want. The attorneys are going to address the material and financial elements of your life together as well as the parenting plan if you have children. They cannot address the emotional and nonmaterial things between you. Your feelings about the divorce and your soon to be "ex-spouse" are yours to manage. Back those feelings out of the discussions and decisions as much as you can. During the back and forth of negotiations emotions can run high.

23

Unchecked, they can motivate you to make bad snap decisions that carry long term negative effects.

Who gets what? The ownership of everything that is a "thing" in your marital home will have to be decided about. You and your spouse are going to create a settlement about who gets what from your shared home. Make a list. Walk through your house, look at everything. It is a good idea to make a video recording or take pictures of the belongings in the house. It is not unheard of for items to disappear during the time when you are negotiating prior to a final settlement. Determine what you would like to keep. Typically, family pieces that came from your side of the family, your jewelry and personal belongings will stay with you. Shared artwork, dishes, pots and pans, furniture, electronics etc. will be divided. It may all seem obvious but assume nothing; especially if you think the other person may get mean or petty or they have a new partner who is trying to influence the process.

After you have determined what things you want to keep, take that same walk, and look at all the things through your spouse's eyes. What things will that person want? This is where you will start to find the things that may cause conflict. It is also where you will find things that can be used to smooth and expedite negotiations. You must be willing to surrender on some things. Being someone who is willing to negotiate, compromise and even concede will look good for you in the eyes of the attorneys and consequently the eyes of the court; it will also minimize the time spent by attorneys going back and forth over things. As ridiculous as it seems, people will spend more money than an item is worth, paying their attorneys to bicker back and forth over who gets the thing. There are very few things that cannot be replaced or lived without; be smart about what you must have. If you can communicate in a civil manner with the other person, either face to face or in writing, divide things up and write it down and submit this to your attorneys. This saves time and money with the attorneys.

If you have a house together, discuss what is best for all regarding that. Is it best that one of you remains in the house? If so, will it be financially viable for the person who stays in the house? Often people want to keep one spouse in the family home so that the kids can keep their home. This is understandable, but if it is not financially feasible, consider letting the house go and both of you getting new places. There is no benefit to one of you keeping the house if you will not be able to maintain a comfortable lifestyle. Holding onto the home for the sake of the kids may feel right in the emotional upheaval of the moment, but if the upkeep is going to become a drain that limits your ability to keep up in other aspects of life, find a more suitable living space. Your children are adaptable and will be happier to see both parties up and functioning in new places without a stoppage in their supply chain. Also setting up new places can help clear the bad air from life.

Divvying up the finances is where you do want to have the experts involved. Do not take the other person's "word for it" and create casual financial arrangements about health insurance, child-care, savings, anything. This is the area where you and your attorney must be clear on what you are entitled to, and how to get that or give that. It may not seem like it now, but your lives will move on, other partners and possibly other children will enter your lives. The financial set up you negotiate needs to be clean and clear, and hopefully fair.

Many women will step back or away from negotiating strongly on their financial behalf because they are focusing on the child aspects of the divorce, or just want to get the process over with. As uncomfortable as you might be, step up and stake your claim for your financial well-being. Your attorney will do the talking here so you have a buffer from the other person when having these discussions. Laws about divorce vary from state to state and even county to county; your lawyer will instruct you as to what you are and are not entitled to in your location. Do not give up what you are entitled to in an effort to appease the other's feelings. Conversely don't get crazy greedy and mean.

If you have changed your name and want to change it back, ask your attorney to add this detail into the final settlement. This is much easier and cheaper than doing it later as an entirely separate legal matter.

Many men will become focused on the financial aspects of the settlement, not paying attention as much to parenting plans and schedules. Often, though not always it is the mother who has been the more hands on parent and the father thinks things with the kids and schedule will just shake out once the divorce is final. If you have a very amicable divorce relationship, they might, but most divorced couples, and certainly the kids, are better off with a clear strong parenting plan. Stay in the negations and use this as a time to begin to see how your parenting responsibilities and expectations are going to change.

This is a negotiation, and you will have to make compromises. You will have to concede some things and fight for others. Don't attempt to punish the other person by trying to shortchange them or put them in a tough spot financially. Don't be sneaky and mean no matter how good it might feel in the moment to think you are sticking it to the other person. That behavior stands to do more harm than good and the spirit of generosity will do more for you in the long run especially if you have children together.

These are emotional times, and decisions about money and possessions can bring out the worst in people. In the end, you both must agree to the terms, and come to a settlement. Dragging things on and on will only be costly on all levels. Negotiate fairly, listen to your attorney, and create a settlement. Once you have arrived at a settlement and have signed off, honor that. Your children are watching and learning, and they will live out firsthand the decisions you make here.

The last bit of the legal process is the filing of the final settlement and going to court. In most cases you will be required to appear at the local courthouse before a judge or magistrate to swear to the validity and acceptance of your settlement. Your attorney will be with you but if you are nervous or anxious ask a friend to go along for support. In the courtroom you will be asked to affirm that you are in agreement with the terms of the settlement. You and your spouse both respond, the document is filed, and you are exes. The funny thing is that if you have children, often the very next thing before leaving the courthouse is a conversation about who is picking up the kids. Life goes on.

Key Management Points

- Negotiation means compromise. Be prepared to compromise and accept that you will not get everything you want.

- Know what is most important to you AND what is most important to the other person.

- Don't shortchange yourself in the process for the sake of the kids or in the belief it will all work out in the end. Get an agreement that is fair.

CHAPTER 5

Money & Finances

"Wealth is the ability to fully experience life."
— HENRY DAVID THOREAU

Divorce costs money, but PLEASE, PLEASE, PLEASE don't let that keep you from taking this step if it is the right way back to wholeness and happiness. Unhappiness has huge costs, monetary and otherwise. Think about the amount of money people spend on a wedding, and that is a one-day event. In 2019 the average cost of a wedding in the US was close to $40,000.00. The average cost for a divorce $15,000.00 per person but there are ways to keep that number down and most attorneys offer payment plans. (See sections on attorneys and negotiation).

From the very beginning of the process, you need to be aware of the financial changes coming your way and manage through them. There are the obvious initial costs like attorney fees and new homes and furnishings. And there are the ones that you may not think of right away that are the result of going from a single household to two. Some people will go from dual income to single income paying support. Others will become single income receiving support. Learn what your particular financial position is likely to be post-divorce and manage to that. Do not let cost keep you from making the right move to divorce, and don't let the change in economics make you bitter and resentful. You can handle this and create a great life for yourself. It may not be the same. It may be a smaller economic footprint than you are used to or ever thought you would have, but you will be surprised at the wealth and well-being that returns to your life that is not about money or things.

Before you meet with your attorney the first time, learn your financial situation if you don't already know it. Learn about your assets **AND** your debts: homes, cars, credit cards, student loans etc. Find out whose name each of these items is in, yours, your spouse's, both? If possible, find and read all the bills and statements. Look up the words and terms you don't know. Learn the difference between good debt and bad debt. You will want to know these things because both assets and debt are going to have to be dealt with. They can be split. They can be assigned to one person or the other. They are going to be part of your negotiation, so the more you know, the better you will be able to negotiate.

If you own a house, whose name is on the mortgage? Find out the current value of the house, and how much you owe. You can go to websites like Zillow or Realtor.com or the website for your area to see homes in your neighborhood to get an idea of the value of yours. Will one of you be staying in the house and buying the other out? How will that impact the finances? Learn the financial facts about your automobiles. Who will get what car or cars? What kind of vehicle will you each need in your new life?

Learn the details about all retirement, investment, and life insurance accounts that you or your spouse have, and what each of your respective rights and claims are to these funds and plans. Is there is other property, vacation homes, collections or hobbies that have cost or value, know about these. Understand your good debt and your bad debt. All of these will be part of the negotiations and final settlement. Look closely and carefully at everything and be prepared. You may find some surprises, good and bad.

If it all seems too confusing and overwhelming your attorney can help with this but learn as much as you can. If you have a good friend or relative who can help you go through all this and get organized, use this person. It is less expensive to make them a nice meal as a thank you than pay your attorney to sort it all out. If this leaves your head spinning and your courage draining, take a break. It will all shake out in the negotiations. Take heart, know your situation, communicate it clearly to your attorney and forge ahead.

Next, if you do not have your own financial profile, you need to create one right away. If you only have shared bank accounts, you need to open a checking account in your own name. Opening an individual account can be tricky if the other person must sign off for you to move money or will be upset if you take money to set up an account in your own name. If you need to do this under the radar, be creative to gather the funds you need to open an account. Sell some things online, borrow money from a parent or family member but do this if you can. Whatever your situation, find a way to do it.

Get at least one credit card in your name, more if you are able. Do some research when you are applying for credit cards. If you have bad credit or are in a shaky financial place, look for companies that are more forgiving. Go online and look for low interest cards. If you get declined for a card, do some research, and find the companies that have the fewest qualifiers. These may be higher interest rates, but the goal is to begin to build your own credit history and to have a credit card handy if you need it. A new credit card in your own name can be the perfect way to afford a retainer for your attorney. Once you get the new card, make small purchases, and pay it off each month. Be aware that opening a new card may lower your credit rating temporarily which is another strong reason to be careful about your spending during this time. However, continue to use the joint ones until you are legally divorced. Be sure to pay attention to your spouse's spending during this time as well. Credit card debt or other debt will be negotiated in your final settlement but less is definitely more in this instance.

The more you can know about your financial life and your rights to your shared assets, the more comfortable you will feel during this part of the negotiation; AND it will set you on the right path for managing your future.

If you are going to receive spousal support or child support, understand how much and the tax implications if there are any. If you are going to have to return to work, or go to full time work from part time, assess the costs of this. Will you be needing childcare? Determine what the cost of this will be and how you and your ex will meet this expense.

Take a full assessment of your financial life and understand what you will need to adjust. Certainly, you want to live comfortably and be able to take care of your children, but you may have to make changes in the way you do this. It could be making changes to the car you drive. If you have a sedan but will now need a minivan, get the minivan (it won't be forever, and you might be surprised to find you like it!). You may have to adjust your budget for clothing, resale clothing is not what it used to be, and you might even sell some of your own items. If dining out was your thing, learn to cook with your kids. It's cheaper and a great way to spend time together. Be prepared to make changes and lead the effort with positivity to your kids. Being happy together eating a meal you prepared together, or watching a movie at home, or game night is priceless.

Knowing and understanding your financial situation will reduce the amount of time your attorneys will need to spend trying to figure it all out and piece it together. Any way you can limit time spent by your attorney is money in your pocket.

The most obvious way of being financially smart at this time is to be mindful of your spending. It is much easier to loosen the financial reigns once you get the hang of your new budget, than to clean up a financial mess made by not paying attention.

Be especially aware of emotional spending. It feels good to do something nice for yourself, especially during these tough times. But that itch, to buy something and "treat yourself" almost always comes back and too many of these moments can add up to a negative financial drain. When you are feeling the urge to buy something to make yourself feel better, slow down and think about what you are feeling. Is the new item really needed, and is it going to truly address your feelings? Sometimes it will but be careful with this sort of spending. You will feel better if you keep your finances in line and become more adept at sorting through your feelings. Try coming up with a new strategy for addressing those feelings in the moment; take a nap, read a book, call and check on a friend, learn something new. A non-monetary distraction will serve the same purpose and be better for you. That itch is really more about nurturing your soul than needing to buy something new.

Knowing your financial situation and getting it and keeping it under control is essential to launching successfully into your new life. Don't be afraid of having less, there is a freedom in having less that you might just find inspiring.

Key Management Points

- Learn everything you can about your shared finances with your spouse.

- Understand your rights to assets and debts.

- Create a independent financial profile if you don't already have one.

- Keep your personal spending under control.

- Accept that your financial situation may take a dip.

- Stability is more important than stuff.

CHAPTER 6

New Home

*"Love begins at home, and it is not how much we
do...but how much love we put in that action."*

— Mother Teresa

Whether you are keeping the place that you and your spouse shared or moving to a new one, you will be setting up a new home. Leaving the home that you set up with such high hopes where you celebrated holidays and birthdays and brought your babies home to can be gut wrenching and one of the hardest parts of the divorce process. You may find yourself walking around the house in a daze. That's ok. You can do that for a bit. If you don't want or weren't expecting the divorce, setting up a new home is probably the last thing you thought you would be doing or want to do. But here you are, set your focus on the task at hand, look forward and put your energy and love into creating this next home.

What makes a strong home, and a happy home is that you feel loved, welcomed, and accepted there. The feeling of "being home" is deep and powerful and while you remember the places, you have called home, it is the *feeling* of home that is so powerful. It is the emotional connection, not the building or the things in it that give the feeling of being home. That comes from the feeling of being loved, supported, and secure in that place. Of course, it is nice to be in a wonderful physical space surrounded by beautiful and comfortable furnishings, but these cannot hold up against what it feels like and means to walk into a home where you are loved and valued. You don't need money and square footage as much as you need heart and courage to set up a new home after divorce.

When you are deciding what to do and where you will live after the divorce, obvious drivers in the decision are money, the kids, proximity to schools and day care, proximity to your ex if you are going to be sharing custody, and your interest in home maintenance. If it's possible to stay in the same neighborhood and school, that is great. If not, don't worry. The kids can adjust, and you will help them do that. A new place can offer a fresh start after divorce for you and your kids.

Understanding where you are going to be financially is key to making the best choice about where to live next, not just the amount of money you will have toward purchasing or renting a place, but the income you will have monthly to live on. Talk to your attorney and get a solid sense of what you can afford. By afford I mean not just the purchase price but the cost of upkeep. If you were not the person paying the household bills in your marriage, learn these costs right away. There are a lot of hidden costs to home ownership like insurance, water, heat and cooling, lawn care, and the entire gamut of home repairs. Keep in mind that once you are in a house it is important to be able to take good care of it to maintain its value.

Determine what you really need and want in your living space, there is a difference between "needs" and "wants", so secure the needs first. Think about how you have been living and what is going to change. What chores are going to come to you now that your spouse is no longer in the picture? If you had someone to help with the house, will you still be able to afford that; if not, smaller houses are easier to keep clean. If you live in a colder climate and hate scraping the windshield on cold mornings, a garage or carport is key. If you love gardening and yard work, find a place that allows for that; if you hate mowing the lawn, and won't be able to afford to have someone to do it for you, forgo the big yard. If you are not a fixer-upper person, don't purchase a fixer-upper house.

Once you have a handle on what you can afford and what you are looking for, go online and start your search. This will help you get an idea of what is available in your price range and area. It's also a great way to think outside the box; expand your search to different types of dwellings and neighborhoods. Look for a place that is well built, affordable, safe, and is a space where you can create a warm and comfortable home. Doing this will build your confidence and educate you before you engage a realtor. Ask people you know if they can recommend a no-nonsense professional realtor. If you don't get a solid recommendation, interview several and be crystal clear with them about your budget and needs. Realtors work on a commission; a bigger sale is a better payday. If they start pushing you beyond your budget, be firm about what you can afford. Ask questions and take the time to educate yourself as you go through the process. If you are in time crunch, for whatever reason, it is almost always better to go smaller and less expensive than to purchase beyond or at the edge of your budget just to get it done. There will be enough changes coming your way; feeling financially strapped by a house is a pressure you do not need. Consider renting an apartment or other place for a while if you cannot find a good fit financially. This is a time in your life when things are changing quickly so landing in an apartment or other rented or leased space may make sense and give you time to get you bearings.

You will have to help your kids adjust at the same time you are adjusting, so keep the communication open. It's not going to be the same so don't tell your kids that it will be. The new place is going to be different, but different doesn't necessarily mean bad. If you and your spouse have been openly hostile and the kids have been living in the middle of that, the new place will definitely be better. Talk to your children about the new place in positive terms. Listen to their concerns and help them through this change. Finding a new home and setting it up is a great opportunity to not just reset, but also to expand your life and your children's lives and doing it together can be a wonderful experience. Make it fun and give them input into appropriate decisions, like the colors in their rooms, new bedding, or finding a new sofa. You can have loads of fun shopping for new things together and creating the new space together is also creating new positive memories.

Plan for your actual move. Moving is one of the hardest things to do, not just emotionally but physically. If you are able engage a professional moving company do it, even if just for the big stuff. The costs of moving can be negotiated into your divorce settlement, or look within your new budget for the funds, it will be worth every penny!

You will probably need or want some new furnishings, and this is a great time to hit the resale shops, antique stores, and flea markets. Conversely, take the things that you no longer need or want in your new home to the resale sale shops or give away to friends or charity organizations. You can bring a lot of life, coziness and fun into your new home without breaking you bank. Don't feel the need to get everything right away; less is often more so go slowly as you furnish your new space.

Sometimes divorce results in not only a new residence, but also a step or two or three, down in the level of living enjoyed when married. Try not to let it bring you down. There is a lot to be said for smaller homes, less yard, new neighbors, and neighborhoods. A smaller building doesn't equate to a lesser homelife. When you are creating your next home, the most important thing is how you and your children and guests feel when they are in your space. It is the love, warmth, laughter, and hospitality that truly make a place a home.

Key Management Points

- Understand your budget for the new home, including all the costs of upkeep.

- It is more important to live comfortably with less financial worry or stress even if this means downsizing.

- You cannot keep everything the same, but you can make it better.

- If you have kids, involve them in setting up the new home in ways that are appropriate and fun.

- Focus on the life of the home, love, safety, warmth, and hospitality.

CHAPTER 7

The Kids

*"Let us put our minds together and see what
life we can make for our children."*

— SITTING BULL

If you have children, they have probably factored heavily into the decision to divorce and may be the reason you have not yet made the move. You have probably had many sleepless nights going over and over this in your mind, "how will my kids deal with two houses? How will they grow up without two parents in the home? Are they doomed to lives of crime and sloth?" Stop this thinking. Your children, just like the rest of humanity, will face changes and tough situations all their lives, what matters right now is your commitment to guide your children through this change. You can do this, and your kids will be better for it.

Parenting means keeping the well-being of your children as a priority in your life. This is true whether you are married or not. But they are not the only priority, you must balance your own wellbeing, work, home, finances, all of it. Being a parent is the world's toughest balancing act with the weights and obstacles always changing. As a parent going through divorce you may feel like you have failed your children by not providing an ideal or perfect childhood. That just isn't the case. There are so many married, "whole" households that are very unstable and unhappy. The family life going on in these homes is far from whole or perfect. Think about your own growing up; if your parents remained married was your childhood perfect? If your parents divorced, were there no good times? Are you irrevocably broken?

Married or divorced, families go through changes and tough times. Families struggle with grave illness, financial difficulties, pandemics, mental health issues, relationship issues, addictions, losses and struggles of all sorts. It is how the family faces the challenges and how they communicate, cope, survive, and even thrive through them that makes the difference. Use this time to teach your children how to positively face life's challenges and keep moving ahead. As the adult and leader of your family, make the decision for yourself and your children that you are going to grow and thrive. This is a life change; a transition and you are going to use it to become stronger, smarter, better people. Assure your children that you will be there to take care of them and guide the process and you are going to continue to be great people. Children are resilient and perceptive, and they are in your slip stream, watching you and taking their cues from you. If you are handling the changes with courage, humor, and pluck, they will feel better and less stressed than if you are crumpled in a ball of despair. You are teaching them how to face life, so model for them how you would want them to face life's challenges. Some days you may have to fake it, but this is time to drive for happiness, even if this change wasn't your decision, because what is your other choice?

Divorce presents different issues for each of you, and it has different challenges for the children depending on how old they are. Believe it or not, divorce is easier for younger children than older ones. Younger children tend get into the swing of the new way of life with less angst. They develop the new relationships dealing with their parents one on one and this becomes the story of how they grow up. They are not working off a "lifetime" of how it used to be with mom and dad, that is not their perspective.

Older children are often caught off guard to find out that their parents are unhappy to the degree of getting divorced. If a bad relationship (whatever version of it you and your ex have been living) is all they have seen and known, they don't know that this isn't how it should be. These older children or adult children often feel when their parents split, like their entire lives were a lie. They can look back at warm memories and those now become a source of confusion. Be available talk and help them sort through these feelings.

If you are one of the many who is waiting for "the kids to be out of the house" to divorce, reconsider that. Many older kids feel guilty that their parent or parents lived unhappily in order to provide them with a "whole" homelife. This is a tough one, and you may have to work on it with your kids for a long time. Talk to them, listen to them, understand their hurt and anxiety. It is not only ok, but also essential to say things like, "I am sorry" and "That must really hurt." You will need to assure them, it wasn't all bad, that many of their memories and perceptions of fun with the family are true and accurate. Encourage them to talk to you, or to a counselor, or other adult or friends. Let them know, that the focus for them should be on moving forward in their own lives.

There are so many things to think about with regard to your children and divorce, it is truly overwhelming. Here are three important things to help you get started on good footing. They need patience and special care and attention:

1. A clear understanding of this adult issue being handled by the adults.

2. The relationship with both parents is a priority for both parents.

3. Mastering the challenge of two homes.

Making these a priority will help with all the others. Remember you must lead to make this work so that the kids can learn to thrive in this new lifestyle.

Number 1

Make it clear that this is an adult issue being handled by the adults and it is not their fault.

The decisions to marry, have children and get divorced are all decisions that were made by adults. And even though the decision to divorce impacts their lives, it is an adult decision and as adults you and your ex are the ones responsible for it. It is so important to make sure your children know that they are not the reason for the divorce, and they cannot fix it. This is not a one-time conversation and it may not stick right away. You will have to keep checking in and reassuring them, maybe for years. Children are in a much smaller mental space than adults, they are the center of their worlds, that is normal, but it means that they bring the events of their lives to that center. You need to bring assurance in your words and your actions, that they are not the reason for the divorce.

Number 2

The relationship with both parents
should be a priority for both parents.

If you are divorcing, the feelings that you once had for the person you married are gone or at the least dramatically different. There is anger, resentment, confusion, and for many of us a strong desire to stick it to the other person. The kids are an easy way to stick it to the other person because the kids are your weak spot. Don't use the kids to stick it to the other person, don't insert your feelings and experiences into the relationship that your kids have with their other parent. The people who get hurt the most when parents use the children as weapons against the other are the children and they have the least coping mechanisms and freedom to deal with the fall out of that. Remember, **it is a completely different thing to be someone's child than to be someone's spouse or ex-spouse.** Think of the relationship with the other parent as something that you actually need to care about and bring through the divorce process intact, not in shreds. Your kids are the people that you say you will do anything in the world for, so be prepared to do some tough things. If it means buying more socks and underwear and swimsuits sure to be lost at the other parent's house do that. If it requires biting off the end of your tongue for the millionth time rather than slinging a mean comment, bite your tongue.

Number 3
Mastering the challenge of two homes.

Transitioning between two homes is full of challenges and you will need to commit to listening and understanding to help your kids become pros at this! Keep at the front of your mind that your kids are going to have to something here that you and your ex will not. Your role here is to assist the kids in all the ways that will help them get up and functioning. To be successful (and success here benefits all parties) moving continually between two homes requires countless gentle reminders, kind notes and text messages, and lots of free passes and forgiveness. Your job here is to eliminate as much stress during the transitions as possible, not add to it. That may seem like an obvious thing but when you are stressed it is easy to start shrieking at the kids over forgotten items, being late or the other parent's slip ups. Losing your cool in these moments only makes everything harder and it will back up on all of you when they become afraid to ask for help or tell you they forgot something. Many things can be duplicated so that they don't have to be carried back and forth, some things cannot. Things that cannot be duplicated you will need to help them to remember and ferry back and forth. Make check lists, send reminders to the child and the other parent, create a routine that incorporates packing up the important things first and learning to double check that you have them before you pull away from the house. When things are forgotten, and they will be, try to keep your cool and go back and get it if you can, or help them cope if you can't, most things can be worked out.

While it may be just the kids physically moving between the two homes, ALL of you have to learn manage the transitions between and existence of two homes. There will now be two places that the kids call home, and the adults must learn to respect the other person's home. Home means, family, expectations, rules, and routines and two homes means two sets of these. No matter how hard you and your ex try you will not always be in synch. This will be even more pronounced because you will parent differently when you are no longer a couple and/or when a new partner and children are introduced. If you and your ex can communicate well and agree on things that pertain to the kids, that is great, the less jarring the differences between the two homes the better. Unfortunately, many co-parents will not or cannot communicate well about the kids and that is stressful on everyone. If you are not able to communicate well, then as much as it may sound counter intuitive creating a distinct line between the two homes can be extremely helpful. It can actually make it easier on the kids because although it isn't a warm fuzzy handoff, it is a clean one and they can learn to enter and exit more easily than slogging through angry driveway transitions.

Discipline is another area ripe for disagreement. You and your co-parent may disagree about punishments such as grounding or taking away electronic devices. It is easiest for all if punishments instituted at one home are carried out at that home. If the other parent agrees and wants to carry that punishment along into their space that is fine, but if not, then let it go. It takes communication and attention to carry punishments between households and is a perfect situation for the kids to play you against each other for their own reasons. Any time you can limit the possibility of arguing between the two households the better for all. Create a system of discipline that includes rewards and punishments for your home and stick to it. Again, people are resilient and adaptable, and you will all adjust. What is most important is to be clear and honest with your children about how things work, what is expected, that you are consistent and that you respect the other parent as much as possible.

There will be differences in the two homes, accept that from the start and help your kids understand that and manage it. The differences will be both positive and negative. It will sting a bit when you learn that there are things your kids really like about the other home. But learn to be happy about that, it is so much better if they are in a place they like. If you cannot be glad about it, then leave that alone, don't disparage or compete. There is no upside to the other home being a negative experience. This is where you must stretch and grow, not easy, but you need to do this for kids as well as yourself. There will also be things they don't like about the other home. This is true in all homes, married or divorced. The hard truth is that, unless the children are being put in harm's way, there is nothing you can do about things you or the kids don't like in the other home, EXCEPT help them to learn to manage the situation.

Support them as needed when they transition. If they need to pack snacks or clothing to get through the time at the other house, help them. If they need a ride to a party or sporting event, offer to provide it. Have their backs. The best possible situation for the kids is smooth transition between the two homes, so as much as you and your co-parent can make it easy, the better.

Divorce definitely changes things for you as a parent, but in the task of raising growing humans, things are always changing. Despite what our culture says, the changes in parenting due to divorce are not all negative. Many parents have much better relationships with their children once the draining task of maintaining an unhappy "married" household is gone. The focus moves from keeping up the appearance or charade, to living life and parenting the kids. Also, because the kids will now be spending long stretches of time with each of you, without the other parent around you can be more fully yourself. The immediate negative interpretation or judgement of the other parent to the kids is dramatically decreased.

Understand from the beginning that what happens at the other person's house, is not under your control and vice versa. You certainly should communicate with the other person on important parenting matters such as school and health and extracurricular activities, but the day in and day out life at the other person's home is no longer yours to participate in. It can take some time to get the hang of this, but unless your children are TRULY being put in harm's way, butt out. Your life will be much easier, and you will have more fun with your kids when you limit the amount of time and energy you give to the other parent's homelife. Your children will do far better managing the different ways of the two homes if you lead with acceptance and kindness rather than rancor and judgement.

Always remember that you are the grown up, you will have to make the best decisions, not necessarily the most popular. But even these decisions will show your children that you are thinking of them and working for what is best. Involve your children in decisions and choices when it is appropriate, but don't when it is not. The goal is to prepare your children to become great adults. Divorce does not change the goal, nor does it necessarily make it harder. It presents new and different challenges, and it eliminates others. It also creates opportunities that would never have presented in your current situation.

Key Management Points

- You are the adult and need to behave as such. It is up to you to lead your kids through this transition with positivity and strength.

- Your kids are resilient and will adapt.

- You need to support the relationship your kids have with the other parent in a healthy manner.

- Communicate frequently with your kids at an age-appropriate level.

CHAPTER 8

Parenting Plans

*"No one should bring children into the
world who is unwilling to persevere to the
end in their nuture and education."*

— PLATO

"No matter how much time you argue to get with your children, there will never be enough time with your children, married or divorced." This insightful statement came from an attorney during negotiations with two parents who were arguing over a 15-minute increment of time. The attorney is right. Children grow up too fast and before you know it your toddlers are grade schoolers, then teens, and then young adults. Divorced or married, they grow up too fast. Divorced or married, your role as parents is to launch your children into adulthood with all the confidence and good sense that you can impart to them to help them to be successful in life.

If your children are under 18 years of age, you will be required to create and file with the court a plan for raising your children with the other parent. Parenting plans are about time, money, and responsibilities and how all of those will be divided/shared in what you and your co-parent determine is in the best interest of your children.

It may seem crazy to ask two people who are not getting along to create a "plan" of any sort, much less one that directs the lives of their children, but there you have it. You have this chance. Use it well. To create a successful parenting plan, think about what is in the best interest of your children and accept that you are going to have to negotiate, compromise and concede to come up with the best plan.

Ideally, you both understand that the issues that ended the marriage are between the two of you and you can put those differences aside when in the parent role. If you can do that but your ex cannot or will not, *you still need to do it anyway*. It is hard to keep an argument going when the other person won't join in. If there are real and genuine issues that involve the safety of the children bring those up to your attorney and get a professional involved. Do this at the beginning of the process and have clear examples and proof. *Differences in parenting style are not considered dangerous or harmful to the court, so don't waste time and money trying to make them seem that they are.*

Your first determination will be what model of co-parenting you are going to do. There are multiple models that differ primarily in the assigning of responsibility. Your attorney will help you to determine what the options are in your location and what is the best fit for you. There can be complete 50/50 sharing or you may determine one of you is best suited to be the "primary" parent. Primary as in the point person, not as in the superior parent.

The financial piece of a parenting plan is the most straight forward, though not easy, piece to work out. As much as possible think through things like health care, education, before and after school care, extra circular activities and fees, holidays, and birthdays, all of these have associated costs. Negotiate for financial support in a way that makes the two homes comparable in terms of what the children need to thrive: food, clothing, medications, electronics etc. The person who has the higher income will be mandated to contribute child support to the other parent's household. Child support is put in place by the courts to minimize the disparity in the standard of living between the households. The person who contributes child support is not exempted from purchasing clothing, food, or anything else that the children will need when they are with them. The person who receives the support payments is not being given fun money to use on themselves. The court expects that the children will have what they need in both homes.

If you are the contributor of child support, don't be resentful, or if you are resentful, don't show that especially to your children. If you are the receiver of child support, be a good steward of these funds. They are meant for use for the lives of children; use them in that way. Do not opt out of the child support system. Do not "wing it" and hope that things will work. As life moves forward other people and children will likely enter your lives and a written and court approved document that addresses these particular children will serve you ALL well.

A genuinely great thing about parenting plans is that creating one forces you to think about the future well-being of your children. If it's possible to establish how you are going to save for college or other future financial support and get that in place now, that is great, you are ahead of the game.

The parenting time schedule is the toughest piece to work out. Talk to people who have parenting plans and learn what is working or not working for them. You have the opportunity to create a schedule that fits the particular needs of your kids, you, and your ex. Look at things from the point of view of ease on the children in terms of school, activities friends and time with both of parents. Make a schedule for the holidays, birthdays, yours as well as theirs, and vacation time. Pay attention to pick-ups and drop-offs, who drives for these and the amount of time that is agreeable to be late. Create fair and workable solutions for lateness or no-shows. It will feel overwhelming and tedious while you are doing it but stick to it. This document will create a structure for your lives that helps to create peace and decrease conflicts. A well-done and thorough parenting schedule respectfully followed goes a long way to smoothing tensions and easing the burden on your kids. As a heads up, when you are completing pick up and drop off plans for schools or activities be specific about who will be doing these. If other people, grandparents, friends or babysitters are involved you must let the organization know this or they will not release your kids to that person.

Of course, as soon as the plan is in place and up and running, there will be times when you or your ex need to adjust. Therefore, it is best if you and your ex can interact well. Obviously its best if you can be civil even friendly to each other, but if that is not possible, then little or no interaction is better than angry and aggressive interactions. It is possible with a good plan to have almost no interaction with the other person at all. This can actually be better for everyone involved than a constant stream of bickering and arguing at pick-ups and drop-offs.

The focus of the parenting plan absolutely needs to be what will make the lives of the children flow and grow. Your goal as a parent, to raise wonderful children into wonderful adults, hasn't changed. Make a plan that gives appropriate time with both parents, minimizes transitions, and assures them that their needs are going to be met. This is time to be a grown up and monitor yourself that you don't try to penalize the other person with decisions made here. There is no middle for you to put the kids in if you do this right by keeping them at the center of the decisions.

Finally, if you are of the belief before the divorce, that the other person is not as good a parent as you, make your peace with that and keep it to yourself. All children, including you and yours, grow up with parents of varying skill sets whether in married households or divorced households. People are not perfect; parents are not perfect; and parenting is hard work. Dig deep. Find your patience, compassion and your common sense. Learn to curb any actions or statements that work against the smoothest running of your parenting plan. And yes, this means that sometimes, or even always you will have to be the bigger person and get over your ex's stupid behavior. Do it for the sake of your kids. You participated in the creation of the parenting plan and signed off on it, so stick to it and use it to establish normal life so that everyone can move forward. If you don't the court has plans and schedules at the ready that can be imposed on your life.

As much as you and your ex-spouse are co-parenting partners, the third co-parent is the court. The court is the monitor of each of you as a parent, you are not the monitor of each other. This third parent partner doesn't want to get involved in your lives unless you cannot manage to parent without them. The odds are extremely high that the other parent is going to make you incredibly angry at times and will do things that you think are wrong and horrible. Who knows, they may be wrong and horrible, or just plain stupid and your kids will be hurt or upset. But you too will stumble and make some bad parenting moves; everyone does, it's part of parenting. That is just the way it is. You must learn to live with it and help your kids learn to live with it. Bad parenting is a fact of life, married or divorced, it is also a choice. Choose to be a good one.

Key Management Points

- A parenting plan allows you to create a framework for parenting with your Ex and a well done one can go a long way to creating calm and respect for all.

- The heart of the parenting plan should be what will be best for your kids, for their daily living and their future.

- To parent well with an ex-spouse you have to accept that you have to accept the way they parent.

CHAPTER 9

Single Parenting

"Trust yourself, you know more than you think you do."
— *Benjamin Spock*

Parenting. It's a cliché but a true one that parenting is one of the most difficult and most rewarding things a person can do. What is it like being a successful single parent? The same as being part of a parenting couple only in **bold**, *italics* and underlined, it is parenting intensified.

Like all other aspects of the divorce process and the establishment of your new life, management of your parenting is essential to getting a handle on the situation. The work of parenting is constant with everchanging circumstance and challenges. Every child will present new and different expectations and needs. This calls for a strong management style. Below are some basic strategies that will help.

Get Organized

Organization is one of the most important things to successful single parenting. If you are an organized person, HOORAY! Hunker down and put all those good habits to work. If you are not an organized person, become one; this is a growth area that will pay off tenfold, so do it, do it now! Organize your house. Have a place for everything: keys, purses, wallets, backpacks, shoes, coats, all of it. Determine a place for everything and work to make putting things in the right place a habit for you and your kids. Establish routines. Have a routine for after school, homework, dinner, bedtime, weekends, and chores. Make lists, reminder notes and texts, all of these

57

cut down on things being forgotten. Place items that must be remembered and reminders strategically in the house, the car, on the bathroom mirror, refrigerator, the way out the door, wherever you will be sure to see them.

Chores

It takes a lot of work to maintain and home and keep a family moving forward. Share the load with your kids. Give your children regular chores and hold them to those. You are the parent, not their servant. There are lots of chores that kids can do: setting the table, sweeping, taking out the trash, doing dishes, putting away groceries, the list is long, and the rewards are many. Chores allow your children to learn how to do basic household tasks, participate in the management of the family and spend time with you. Regular chores also help you to create the routine and this then helps them ease back into your household. Choose chores that they can be successful at and praise them for a job well done. Will they fuss and object and procrastinate? You bet they will, enjoy that, it's normal!

Fun

Make it fun. Fun is an often overlooked power tool in the parenting arsenal. Why not? Life is going to throw plenty of tough days and tough times at your children, so why not make some fun when you are together. It doesn't have to be a big deal or cost money; it can be simple like taking a walk to the store for a slushy or just ice cream for dinner. Making a camp in the living room with blankets or painting together with watercolors or a spontaneous karaoke party can be the source of a great time and wonderful memories. It goes by so fast, have some fun!

Rest

Take a nap. Getting over tired is a sure way to end up getting impatient and angry with your kids. This will typically result in you saying or doing something that you regret, when really all you needed, and probably your kids too, is a little rest. Take a nap, go to bed early, sleep in a little bit. It is amazing how much good a little sleep can do.

Accept Help

You got divorced; you didn't transform into a superhero. You don't have to do everything by yourself. It is ok to accept help when it is offered and even ask for it when you need it. If you need an extra hand with the yard work, household chores or picking up the kids, ask a friend, pay a neighbor kid, or hire a professional. Getting assistance is far better than exhausting or injuring yourself or making a mess of something because it was too much to handle alone.

Expectations

Take a moment and think of all the people you know who had a perfect childhood. There are people who had great ones, and people who had awful ones, but not a soul had a perfect one. Of the folks on the good list, none of them are there because their parents were married and some on that list had parents who divorced. The expectation of creating a perfect childhood for kids is simply unrealistic and unattainable for ALL parents. Your expectation of yourself as a parent should be high and should remain so when you divorce, but also keep it realistic and attainable. You are going to do some really stupid things as a parent, but you will do some great ones too!

Guilt Management

There is a tendency among divorced parents to feel guilt toward their children about the divorce. This whole line of thinking is usually tangled and murky and unfortunately tends to lead to some poor parenting choices. There are parents who wait on their kids like slaves, buy them expensive electronics and clothes and toys and have no expectations or consequences for bad behavior. The reason they give is, "It's because of the divorce, I just feel so guilty..."

You owe your kids the best you can do as a parent to launch them into adulthood. When you weave guilt over the divorce into the essence of your lives it skews things. You are also allowing guilt to have more power in your life as a parent than normal common-sense parenting.

If you feel guilty, talk to a counselor, read a book about it. Don't saddle your kids and your life with guilt. It won't have a positive influence, and it's just too heavy; for all of you. Guilt creates confusion, low self-esteem, sadness and anger not healthy parent child relationships.

Once you get organized and get the hang of the new schedule, things will start to fall into place and before you know it you will have a new normal. If you are co-parenting, you will have mastered the fine art of the pick-up and drop-off. And before you know it, you will find yourself happy when your kids are with you and sometimes even feel happy to see them go. And your kids will feel the same!

Key Management Points

- Single parenting has the same goal as married parenting, raise wonderful children into great adults.

- Organization and routines are key to creating a calm and productive homelife.

- Take care of yourself so you can take care of the kids.

- Keep your expectations strong but also realistic.

- Make it fun your kids will grow up fast. Have as much fun as you can while you can.

CHAPTER 10

Breaking The News

"Be sincere, be brief, be seated."
—Franklin D. Roosevelt

Telling people that you are getting divorced can be a tough conversation. You may find that you are dreading it so much you decide to not have it and just let people find out. You are already feeling raw and vulnerable so initiating conversations about your divorce is not going to be on the top of your list of things you want to do. This is completely understandable, and you don't need to rush to tell people who are not in your immediate family or closest circle of friends. It is fine to let those you aren't close to find out through others. The best course of action is to tell your children and family and close friends before they hear it from someone else. If you and your spouse are getting along at this point get together and agree on how you want to start breaking the news. People talk, and once the news gets out, it is going to start to spread without you being able to have any control over it.

If you have made the decision to leave the marriage on your own tell your spouse first. Some people get so excited or anxious once they have made the decision to divorce that they start telling people and engage an attorney before they tell their spouse! Don't do this. It has the potential to make the other person feel betrayed and humiliated. Go ahead and research attorneys, but please, unless your attorney advises you differently, tell your spouse first. You are going to be connected to this person for the rest of your lives if you have children, so the less animosity you create, the better for all. The negotiation process is much easier if you treat each other with respect. Let the other person be the first to know your decision to divorce is a great way to start.

Give some thought to how you are going to break the news to your children. Hopefully the two of you can agree about how to do this. Many parents will have this discussion with their children together, presenting a united front about splitting. If you think that will work, great. But if the kids have been living with the two of you in a state of constant discord and disconnect, approaching them together, about splitting may be very confusing. It may work just as well or even better, to have one person tell them, and the other to follow up very soon with more conversation. This eliminates the possibility of the discussion becoming another uncomfortable argument for your kids to witness. It also allows you both to speak more freely. Whatever you decide to do, do it. Don't run the risk of them hearing it from someone else.

When you have this conversation with your children, talk to them in age appropriate language and do not overwhelm them. If you are not sure what is age appropriate ask a counselor or teacher or look it up online or in a book. Present plain facts in simple language. Tell them what they can expect and that they are going to be taken care of. Be honest in your explanation the situation and reasons for it as much as they are able to understand. Be prepared with what you are going to say and stick to it. It is highly likely they will be upset so be ready and quick to offer comfort and assurance. Don't digress into blaming the other person, and don't give details that are too adult or private. No matter how blisteringly upset and hurt you are, no matter how much you want to trash the other person to the kids, don't do that.

This is time for you to be the grown up and to be in loving control of the information. Let them ask questions and give them honest answers. Prepare for and encourage ongoing conversation and discussion. What they are going to want and need to know is that it is not their fault, that they will be well taken care of, and that life is going to be fine possibly, likely, even better.

If your children ask you if you are getting divorced, before you have a chance arrange a conversation, answer them honestly. If you say no in that moment because you were planning to tell them later, you are giving them a dishonest answer that will be confusing. Say yes and have the conversation or have an abbreviated version of it and follow up.

Let your children know that you will tell their teachers and coaches. When you do this give those adults all the new contact information and addresses for both of you. Ask the schools to begin communicating with both of you about school events and issues with your children. Give the school a copy of your parenting schedule. You can even make a simple schedule for the school that shows who is responsible for pick up and drop offs each day. For most children divorce means transitioning between two homes and teachers can be a great assist for kids if they know that is what is happening. If your children participate in extracurricular activities, let those adults know as well.

Talk to your children about how they want to tell their friends. If they would prefer that you handle this communication through the parents of their friends do that. If your child doesn't not to talk to friends about it right away, ask the other families to honor that. A friend whose parents are divorced, could be a great resource to your child and to you. If your children are older encourage them to tell their friends in their own way. Or you can offer to practice with them how they want to share this with friends. They don't have to share more than they are comfortable with, but they will do better being in control of this information, just as you are.

Family and close friends need to hear it from you. Just as with your kids, prepare for these conversations. Give honest information, but not too much. You don't have to give all the explicit details even if you are asked. Hold back from trashing the other person as much as you are able. This is a very personal experience that has a very public aspect to it so it needs strong management. Less is more in this situation. Do not share information with anyone that you don't want shared with others. Most people will say that they keep things to themselves, and many do, but many do not. Share what you would be comfortable overhearing others saying about your divorce at the grocery.

At work let your boss know, especially if you are going to need time away for meetings with your attorney or court dates. If you are the boss, make sure that your close colleagues are aware about what you are going through. Alert human resources for things like name change, health insurance, life insurance beneficiaries etc. Just as in your personal life, you are going to do better if you get the news out the way you want and to the people that you want to know. Not sharing the news then falling apart at work or having your work suffer without your colleagues knowing what you are going through, is much tougher to deal with than conversations that you initiate.

Tips for These Hard Conversations
Be Honest

Being honest doesn't mean you need to share everything. Keep it short. You don't need to tell everyone everything about your life or your ex's life. You are better served if you don't. You can share more as you get your footing, but you cannot un-share.

Control the Conversation

If conversations get sticky, if people are asking questions you don't want to answer, or the conversation is becoming too emotional, stop the conversation. One simple way to change the topic of conversation is to redirect it from your divorce to them; this almost always works as people prefer to talk about themselves. Or you can politely say you don't want to talk about it anymore. If this is awkward for you, a great trick is to pretend you are getting a call from someone and take the call, this allows you to politely excuse yourself and walk away. Just because someone asks you a question, doesn't mean you must give them an answer. Learn to redirect the conversation.

Be Prepared

Be prepared for anger, confusion, resentment, sadness from children, family, and friends. But also, be prepared to hear that people are glad you are getting divorced. Sometimes that is the most maddening and surprising thing: to get the feedback, "It's about time!" You may even get this response from your children. Don't take this personally, take it as a validation of the decision. Get the news out and get back to paying attention to all the other things you need to do to get through the process. People talk, the news will spread.

Key Management Points

- The news that you are getting divorced should come directly from you to those you are closest to and will be most impacted by the change.

- When you tell your children, be honest and age appropriate. Let them ask questions and express concerns and talk to them frequently about the decision and the changes.

- You need to inform people in your life you are getting divorced; you don't need to bare your soul to everyone.

CHAPTER 11

The Ex

*"The best revenge is to be unlike him
who performed the injury."*
— Marcus Aurelius

*"Some of us think holding on makes us strong,
but sometimes it is the letting go."*
— Herman Hesse

How to deal with, relate to, or just be in the same room with your "soon to be ex" is an important thing to consider and manage. This person, who at one time in the past was the person you pledged to go to the end your life with, is now moving to the category of "ex" spouse. This transition in one sense happens quickly, in an instant, at the moment one or both of you decide to end the marriage, but also it is a slow metamorphosis. This process of change is one of the strangest and most personally perplexing parts of getting divorced. The person you couldn't wait to see has become a person you barely recognize, or perhaps someone you see all too clearly. And just as that person is becoming your ex, you are becoming theirs.

If you don't have children, you can put this person in your history fairly quickly. Once the divorce is finalized you are free to never deal with this person again; and if you must for whatever reasons, you can keep your distance.

If you have children be mindful that this person will continue to be a part of your life. While the children are still young you may have to interact almost daily. As the kids get older the amount of interactions will lessen but that person will be there, if even just on the periphery, for the rest of your life. Therefore, how you interact with this person during the divorce process is important. The time to lay the groundwork for the future is now.

Married people share a life, a commitment to the marriage, and good or bad there is a marriage bubble in which you exist. Within that bubble there is a certain level of shared privacy and privilege to each other's intimate life. Even couples who are not getting along tend to protect that reality to a certain degree. You are seeing each other day in and day out, you have grown accustomed to each other's habits and quirks. For some there is a shared bond of enduring the bad marriage, for the kids, or for appearances, but a bond, nonetheless. The advent of divorce bursts that bubble and that bond. This is no longer the person that you can "say anything to" or let your hair down around. Start to monitor your interactions with this person as if you were a fly on the wall watching how these two people interact and hold yourself to a high standard. Stick to the Golden Rule, it is a tried and true standard that will benefit you in the present and in the long run. And remember the **Golden Rule is to treat others as you would like to be treated, not as they have treated you, BIG difference.**

You may feel that your soon to be ex is the world's biggest jackass who DOES deserve revenge and at the very least a piece of your mind, and you are going to give it to her/him if it's the last thing you do! It is exactly because of this level of emotion, maybe all it justified, that you need to diffuse.

Bend the ear of a close friend with your plans for retribution. If you keep a journal, write it all down. Take a run. Blast your music. Do something other than the dastardly thing you want to do because even if that person deserves it, acting on this will not help in the big picture. It is normal and natural to have strong negative feelings and wish the other person all manner of revenge and grief. But consider yourself warned. Taking out your negative feelings on your ex almost always creates more negative than positive results. Doing things like putting itching powder in their under-wear, destroying personal items, trashing them to the kids, friends and family or whatever else you might think they deserve can feel wonderful and cathartic in the moment, but how is it going to look to the attorneys and to your children? You might be unpleasantly surprised to find yourself viewed as a wrathful crazy person rather than the long-suffering victim. Does wreaking havoc on the other person help you establish a better and healthy new life?

Be mindful, be careful, be smart. There is an old expression "Let go or be dragged" and it is going to serve you well here. Even if you didn't want the divorce, let the person, the anger, and the hurt go; or you will be dragged.

Key Management Points

- Employ the Golden Rule as the guide to how to treat your ex. The Golden Rule is to treat others how you would like to be treated, NOT reciprocating bad treatment.

- Letting go frees you up for getting on to the next phase of your life. "Let Go, or Be Dragged." Zen Proverb

CHAPTER 12

New Relationships

*"And suddenly you know: It's time to start something
new and trust the magic of beginnings."*
— MEISTER ECKHART

*"It's all right letting yourself go, as long
as you can get yourself back."*
— MICK JAGGER

Wow! New relationships, new romance, this is heady stuff. This is
a guidebook for getting through divorce, not a guide to relationships. Therefore, what you will find here are some basic guidelines
to consider as you re-enter the world of relationships and romance.
If you want more than what you find here, there are literally thousands of books about relationships and every aspect of them, so
do a little reading, or if you have a counselor talk to that person
or talk to your friends.

Divorce is the termination of this marriage; it is not the end of
romance or relationships in your life. As this marriage ends, you may
find yourself super excited to find a new love, you may be feeling
energized and a renewed sense of freedom or you could be feeling
cynical and burned thinking NEVER AGAIN! Whatever, you are
feeling, you will benefit by using this marriage and its ending as a
learning tool for understanding more about yourself and what you
want, need and are willing to bring to a new relationship.

You are a different person than when you married. Take a good
look at who you are now and what was missing or what went wrong
in the marriage relationship. As difficult as it is, look at yourself
and be gently honest as well as complimentary. It is easy to simply

blame the other person, but that won't give you much in the way of understanding yourself or your future. You have changed and grown. What qualities are important to you in a partner now? Do you even want a partner, or are you happier to simply have some companionship now and then? It takes time for the dust to settle, so don't hurry into something permanent.

Check in with yourself as time moves along. You will find that you keep changing as you move further from your marriage and the more you get to know yourself.

Two Important Things to Give Attention
Safe Sex

This may seem obvious, but if you are out of practice or swept up in the wave of an exciting new romance, it is easy to forget or overlook the necessity of safe sex. After being in an unhappy or unfulfilling relationship, re-entering the world of dating can be a heady experience. For many it's like getting out of jail. You have just come through or are coming through an emotional upheaval, and a new emotional and physical relationship can be invigorating, healing and wonderful. BUT an unplanned pregnancy or a sexually transmitted disease can really take the bloom off things, so take care of these matters. Some people make the decision to permanently end their reproductive capabilities. If you are at a point in your life that you know you do not want to have more children, give this some consideration. This seems a choice most often taken by people whose children are already grown or are a bit older and don't want to start with babies again. However, you may meet someone who does want children, so give this option ample consideration. Understand that you still need to be careful about sexually transmitted diseases. You are a grown up so there is no excuse not to handle this responsibly.

Dating and the Kids

Before you start dating think about how you are going to handle dating and new people with your children. Some people make a rule that they will never introduce anyone they are dating to their children. Their thinking is that this is too hard on the kids to see their parent with another person. That is understandable and makes sense. It is a good practice not to introduce your children to every first date, that would be confusing. On the other hand, why not introduce someone you have met and are going out with to your kids? Your children know that you are divorced, therefore single. Your children are your family, and they want and deserve to know what is going on in your life. Most kids very much want their parents to be happy after the divorce. If you are happily dating someone who brings positive energy and life to you there can be a benefit to your children in meeting that person. The key is to communicate honestly with your children about your dating status. Don't spring a new person on them without a discussion. This can create an awkward or hard situation for them and that person. Don't create a revolving door of new people. This is a recipe for embarrassing moments for all. Talk to your kids. Be honest. Be positive. Listen to their concerns. Keep it age appropriate and don't share too much, you are the parent and need to maintain appropriate boundaries. Give them time to adjust to the idea of your dating and proceed at a pace that makes the experience positive for everyone. The introduction of new people and the conversations around that can also give great insight to how your kids are feeling about the divorce and relationships.

If you have decided that it is too much for your children to know that you are dating, give this a bit of thought. They will probably figure out you are dating and will ask you about it. You don't want to lie, that will come back on you. It's a better thing to communicate with them about what your life, and your ex's life are going to be like now that you are divorced. It would be much more jarring to suddenly introduce someone that you are entering into a long-term relationship with than to have met that person and known about for a while. Dating is normal and usually fun. It is a part of life that your children will one day engage in or may already be doing. The key here is to communicate; talk AND listen. Just as you were modeling adult relationships to your children when you were married, you are doing that when you date; be mindful of what examples you are setting. If you are dating someone who you believe simply meeting will be detrimental to your children, reevaluate why you are spending any time with this person.

A Little Friendly Advice

A. When you are ready to have some companionship in your life the abundance of online dating sites makes it easy to find someone to date very quickly. That is great. Get out there and enjoy all the fun things that dating has to offer; but manage yourself. If you go a little over the top, don't worry, lots of people do. If you go out on some dates and find you aren't ready, stop. There are plenty of wonderful ways to spend your time besides dating.

B. Absolutely understand that people are watching, talking, and sadly, judging. It is amazing how people with talk, and the wild inaccuracies that they will be willing to repeat, even your good friends. For your own peace of mind manage your dating situation with discretion. It will serve you well.

C. Don't bring your ex up in conversation on your dates, especially the first one. If you don't want to be with that person anymore, you can be darn sure your date doesn't either. If you are still so angry or bruised from the marriage and the divorce, that you cannot get through a first date without unloading about your ex, you probably need a bit more time to reconnect with yourself before dating. If you are carrying hypersensitivity to mannerisms, expressions or likes and dislikes that your spouse had and those upset you or set you off a person, again, hold off a bit before jumping back in the pool.

D. It is a lot to end a marriage, whether you wanted to end it or not. Either way there is plenty of dust, let it settle. There is a huge benefit to standing on your own after your marriage ends. That doesn't mean that you shouldn't date or try new relationships but take your time before you commit to a new permanent relationship. If you have already met a new partner and that relationship was the catalyst for ending your marriage, you still may want to take some time before committing to a new marriage. You will be glad you did and if the new person is the right person, they will support you in that.

On that same note – life is full of surprises and love unfolds in all sorts of ways and sometimes when you least expect it. Use your common sense and what you have learned from your marriage and the divorce process to proceed with positive confidence.

Embrace the time you have now to be on your own. There is nothing wrong with nights or weekends on your own. You are not alone; you are spending time with you. For all the times you said, "I wish I just had some time for myself," well now you do, don't waste it! Get going on all the things you wished you had time to do!

Finally, as much as it sounds cliché, THE most important new relationship at this time, and always, is the one you have with yourself.

Key Management Points

- New relationships are exciting and fun but need management.
- Safe sex is essential.
- Communicate with your kids honestly about dating.
- The relationship that needs the most attention right now is the one you have with yourself.

CHAPTER 13

New Life – New You

"Wherever you go, there you are."

— BUDDHA

You are going to learn so many things about yourself and your life when you go through divorce! You may find that when you look back on the person you were when you married, you hardly recognize that person now. The process of divorce will confront you with change on all levels of life: personally, spiritually, emotionally, financially, physically, socially. When everything in your life changes, you change. What those changes are and who you grow into is in your control. You may feel like nothing is in your control right now and you may not want to learn lessons or grow. Change of this magnitude can be exhausting and difficult and just really suck. It can make you feel like every decision and choice you ever made was wrong and now you question your ability to make even simple decisions. Everything is in flux and every day is full of new challenges and changes. This means that the constant in life is you. The place to find and create the certainty in your life now is in you; your heart, your mind, your choices.

Initially you will probably find that you have more time to yourself. Instead of seeing this as a bad thing, look at it as time with yourself and use this time to think about and create a new way of living that you love. That sounds heady and philosophical and it is. You have this opportunity to hit the pause button and take stock. Think about who you are, and who you were before you were married. What have you learned about yourself (good and bad)? How have you changed (good and bad)? Don't shy away from the bad stuff. Being honest with yourself and facing the uglier aspects of your personality and the way you live can yield some of the most valuable information for creating a new life. You will see things you want to change or eliminate and things you want to develop and grow!

Your morals and values are your strong foundation, so check in with them and use them to guide you through these days. If you aren't sure what your foundational beliefs are and have been just floating along or got those from your ex, it's time to give the deeper aspects of life your attention. If you aren't sure how to do this, you can talk to friends, check out a faith community, take a class, read some books, watch movies that address the larger questions of life.

This is a wonderful time to find a new hobby or dive back into an old one. If you have always wanted to learn something, do that now! Take a class if you can. Learn things online. If you are returning to work or must work more, try something different. Spend time and energy on yourself.

Take good care of yourself. Rest, exercise, have fun. It may be hard at first so put selfcare into your daily routine. Sit down to a nice dinner every night, even if you are home alone. Go to bed on time. Wake up, get up, get dressed, and get going. Go out to dinner, movies, flea markets, weekend trips alone. You will be surprised how much fun you have with your own good company. Sure, there will be days when you are feeling so sad and lost that you just can't get out of bed and one or two of those is ok, but then get on with it. These are your days, make the most of them, you are so worth it.

Key Management Points

- This is a time of tremendous opportunity for personal growth and development.
- Use this time of change to touch base with your foundational beliefs and values.
- With more time on your own use it to learn things and do things you have always wanted to do.
- Plan your time when the kids are away.
- Take good care of yourself.

CHAPTER 14

Resources for the Journey

"The adventure of life is to learn.
The purpose of life is to grow.
The nature of life is to change.
The challenge of life is to overcome.
The essence of life is to care.
The opportunity of like is to serve.
The secret of life is to dare."

— WILLIAM ARTHUR WARD

As with any change or transition there are rough patches when you find yourself overwhelmed. It is normal to feel fearful and out of control and this can lead to feeling sad and lonely. All of a sudden, the routines of life are different, the people you see and interact with regularly have changed. One of the hardest adjustments to make is finding yourself with a lot more time alone. Weekends, evenings, and holidays that used to be populated by children, and family life have become long stretches of quiet and emptiness. This can be fertile ground for the blues.

Sometimes being sad is good and right thing to do. You are going to have to mourn this loss, so take the time to do that. But sadness can stick around too long and show up too often. Obsessive thinking can not only suck up time, but it can also make problems where there are none. Like the other aspects of this journey, you must manage your emotional life. If you find however that you are sinking into despair and you just cannot get going, seek professional help. There is no shame in needing assistance and the sooner you get help the sooner you will feel better.

Here are some tried and true resources that can work for keeping your spirits up and your face pointed toward the sun. Most require little financial investment and those that do, don't need much. The benefit of all of them is that they break the cycle of sad thoughts or obsessive thoughts thus making room for fresh air, light, and growth. Even something that takes just a little bit of time a day can make a huge positive impact.

Laugh

The power of laughter cannot be overstated. Set a goal to laugh at least once a day and make sure you do it. Watch funny movies or comedians. If you have kids, make sure to laugh with them.

Get a Hobby

Hobbies are such a wonderful contributor to mental health and fun living. You can reinvigorate an old hobby or start a new one. Taking the time to invest in something that is interesting to you is an incredibly positive thing and also gets you connected with people who share your interests.

Take a Nap

New routines, new homes, new situations are exhausting. Sometimes when everything seems bleak or overwhelming that is because you are exhausted. Take a nap. Even a 20 min power nap can be just the thing to chase away those low energy blues and jumpstart the day.

Music

Music is such a healing and life-giving force. Crank it up! Beware though, music can also be a trigger to deep emotions and memories. If you are suddenly sucked into a sad memory or emotional black hole by a piece of music or a song, turn it off. You have the controls, use them! Stick to the music that lifts your spirits.

Get Moving

Whatever your thing is: running, swimming, walking, dance, aerobics, archery, hiking, kayaking, golf, softball, skiing, rollerblading, ice skating, soccer, or croquet, get moving. Combine these with music for a double burst of positive energy. Some activities are going to put you out among other people, another double the benefit. This is also a great time to learn a new physical skill. Get a used bike with a basket and start to do close errands on the bike. Sand volleyball is becoming more and more popular. If we are still dealing with the pandemic, hiking, running and golf are perfect to be outdoors with others social distanced or alone.

Read & Write

Read, read, read! Read stories, read poetry, read magazines, read about things you are wondering about, just take some time to read. Read to be entertained, read to learn, and by all means read with your children! Listening to books is wonderful too and there are lots of inexpensive services for this.

Keep a journal and write your heart out. Write short stories, poems, letters. Write for the fun of writing.

Learn Something New

Whether it is a new sport, hobby, recipe, language, skill, or craft, learning something new always lifts you out of the mindset you were in and takes you some place new.

Friends

Reach out to your friends. The divorce process will have you very self-focused. Reach out and reconnect to your friends, check in on them and put the focus on them. Reaching out is a great cure for too much looking in.

If you lost friends in the course of your divorce now is the time to make new friends. If you have met some nice people at support groups during the process, invite one of them on a hike or for coffee. People who have been through divorce can be great new friends because they can empathize with what you have gone through. But divorce doesn't have to be the touch point for a new friend. Think of people you have met at school, work, church, or in the community that you have thought you would like to know better and make a plan to get to know them.

Self-Care

Check in with yourself and put the focus on you. Do something nice for yourself. The old saying that you won't be able to take care of others, if you don't take care of yourself is true. Take a bubble bath, watch movies that make you feel good, light candles and enjoy a book with your favorite treat, get a new haircut, get your car washed and detailed, get a new bathrobe or towels, make an indulgence purchase of quality soap or skin care, get braces. Whatever it is that you need, do that for you.

Notes to Self

Sometimes your mind needs a nudge to take it out of a repetitive thought cycle. Being alone in the house makes it easy to slip into these mental ruts and harder to get out. Put notes up around your house with reminders to think of people or things that make you happy or with lists of things you want to do. Post them on the mirrors, the coffee maker, any spot where you will see them. You are your own best manager for your mental and emotional content. Create a habit of positive mental content and strength.

Pets

Adding a pet to your life can be a HUGE benefit. Dogs can get you out and walking on a regular basis and cats too are great company.

Consider a cat or dog from a rescue agency and consider an older or senior animal. These guys are often already housebroken and used to functioning with a family. Find the pet that is a good fit for you. But if you don't have the time or the infrastructure to care for a pet don't now is not the time to get one.

Key Management Points

- This is a very emotional time in your life, it is easy to fall into the blues. It will take attention, management, and work to get through it not just intact but better.

- Take simple positive steps and engage in healthy activities to get through these times.

- Remember, you are not alone, you are with YOU! Enjoy the time while you have it, it probably won't last long.

Quotations Cited

1. Proulx, E. Annie. The Gigantic Book of Famous Quotations, p 39. Kelly, Joanne. November 2020.

2. "Joan Rivers" AZQuotes.com. Wind and Fly LTD. 2020. 29 December 2020. https://www.azquotes.com/quote/246386

3. Bender, Betty. The Gigantic Book of Famous Quotations, p 607. Kelly, Joanne. November 2020.

4. Smith, Angela Deavere. The Gigantic Book of Famous Quotations, p 93. Kelly, Joanne. November, 2020.

5. Bragan, Bobby. The Gigantic Book of Famous Quotations, p 95. Kelly, Joanne. November 2020.

6. France, Anatole. The Gigantic Book of Famous Quotations, p 81. Kelly, Joanne. November, 2020.

7. Lindbergh, Anne Morrow. The Gigantic Book of Famous Quotations, p 81. Kelly, Joanne. November, 2020.

8. Sitting Bull. Public Domain.

9. Proverb. Public Domain.

10. Teasdale, Sara. The Gigantic Book of Famous Quotations, p 31. Kelly, Joanne. November, 2020.

11. Eliot, Robert. The Gigantic Book of Famous Quotations, p 31. Kelly, Joanne. November, 2020.

12. Thoreau, Henry David. Public Domain.

13. "Mother Teresa." AZQuotes.com. Wind and Fly LTD. 2020. 29 December 2020. https://www.azquotes.com/quote/292123

14. Plato. Public Domain.

15. "Benjamin Spock." AZQuotes.com. Wind and Fly LTD. 2020. 29 December 2020. https://www.azquotes.com/quote/280007

16. "Franklin D. Roosevelt." AZQuotes.com. Wind and Fly LTD. 2020. 29 December 2020. https://www.azquotes.com/quote/250920

17. Aurelius, Marcus. Public Domain.

18. Hesse, Herman. Public Domain

19. Eckhart, Meister. Public Domain

20. "Mick Jagger." AZQuotes.com. Wind and Fly LTD. 2020. 29 December 2020. https://www.azquotes.com/quote/1144111

21. Buddha. Public Domain.

22. "William Arthur Ward." AZQuotes.com. Wind and Fly LTD. 2020. 29 December 2020. https://www.azquotes.com/quote/386533

About the Author

Sara Jacobs is twice divorced currently single. She holds a master's degree in theology and has worked professionally as an adjunct instructor at the University of Cincinnati and Xavier University and as an executive assistant and office manager. She makes glass beads and jewelry, is a voracious reader and loves to cook. Sara is the mother of two amazing adult daughters, and currently resides happily with her dogs and cat in Cincinnati.

Follow Better Not Broken on Instagram at:
betternotbroken_divorceguide